# How to Draw Egypt Step-by-Step Guide

Best Egypt God Drawing Book for You and Your Kids

BY

## ANDY HOPPER

© 2019 Andy Hopper All Rights Reserved

# Copyright Notes

The material in question, hereto referred to as The Book, may not be reproduced in any part by any means without the explicit permission of the bearer of the material, hereto known as the Author. Reproduction of The Book includes (but is not limited to) any printed copies, electronic copies, scanned copies or photocopies.

The Book was written as an informational guide and nothing more. The Reader assumes any and all risk when following the suggestions or guidelines found therein. The Author has taken all precautions at ensuring accuracy in The Book but assumes no responsibility if any damage is caused by misinterpretation of the information contained therein.

# Table of Contents

Introduction .................................................................... 4

How to draw Horus ....................................................... 5

How to draw Mut ......................................................... 20

How to draw Anubis .................................................... 35

How to draw Osiris ..................................................... 50

How to draw Bastet .................................................... 63

How to draw Ra .......................................................... 78

How to draw Amon-Ra ............................................... 93

About the Author ..................................................... 106

# Introduction

Kids have this intense desire to express themselves the ways they know how to. During their formative years, drawing all sorts is on top of their favorite things to do. You ought to encourage as it boosts their creativity and generally advances their cognitive development.

This book is written to give you and your kids the smoothest drawing experience with the different guides and instructions on how to draw different kinds of objects and animals. However, you should note that drawing, like everything worthwhile, requires a great deal of patience and consistency. Be patient with your kids as they wade through the tips and techniques in this book and put them into practice. Now, they will not get everything on the first try, but do not let this deter them. Be by their side at every step of the way and gently encourage them. In no time, they will be perfect little creators, and you, their trainer.

Besides, this is a rewarding activity to do as it presents you the opportunity of hanging out with your kids and connecting with them in ways you never knew was possible. The book contains all the help you need, now sit down with them and help them do this.

That is pretty much all about it - we should start this exciting journey now, shouldn't we?

# How to draw Horus

# Step 1.

Draw a small circle at the top of the head sheet.

# Step 2.

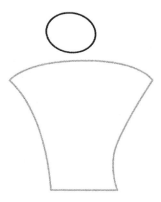

Draw a trapezoidal body just below the head.

7

# Step 3.

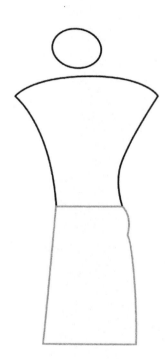

Draw a skirt just below the body.

# Step 4.

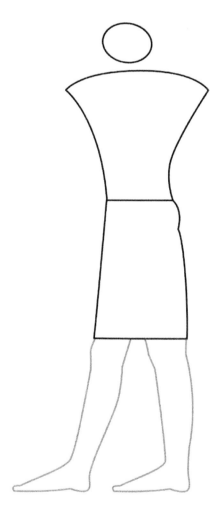

Add two legs to the profile under the skirt.

# Step 5.

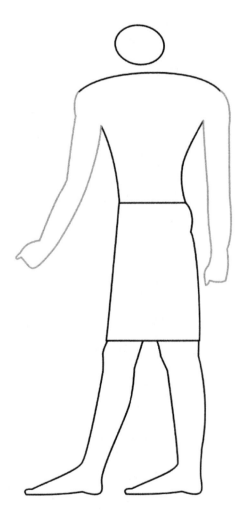

Add two hands on the sides of the body.

10

# Step 6.

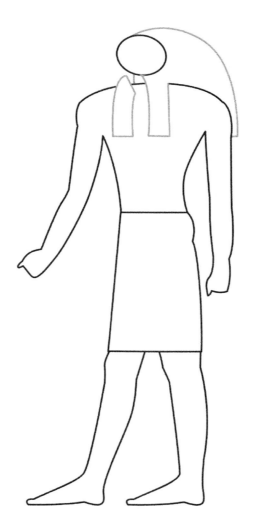

Draw a hairstyle, as shown in the example.

# Step 7.

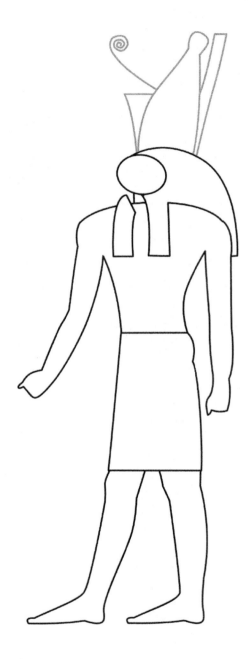

Add a hat to the head.

# Step 8.

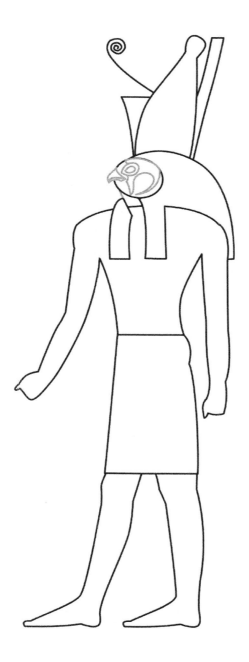

Draw the face of the princes in profile.

13

# Step 9.

Add jewelry in the form of bracelets, necklaces and belts.

# Step 10.

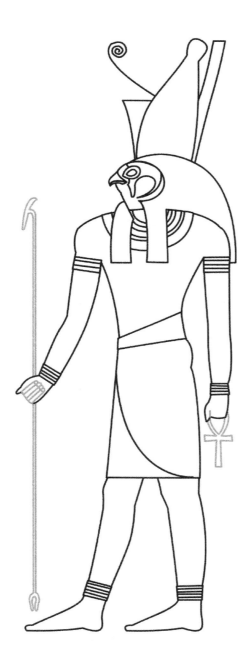

Draw a staff and ankh cross in the hands of Horus.

15

# Step 11.

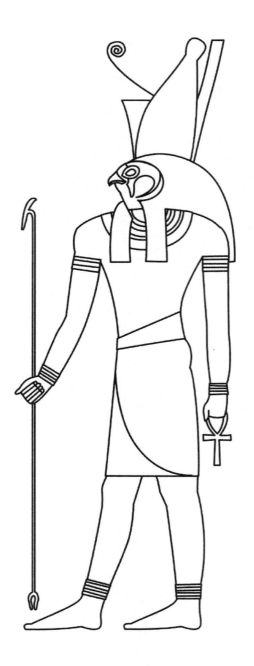

Done, let's start coloring!

# Step 12.

Color picture using brown for skin, dark blue for hair and staff, white for hat and face, yellow for skirt and decorations.

# Step 13.

Add some shadows and highlights to add volume.

18

# Step 14.

Colored version.

# How to draw Mut

# Step 1.

○

Draw a small circle at the top of the head sheet.

# Step 2.

Draw a long dress, as shown in the example.

22

# Step 3.

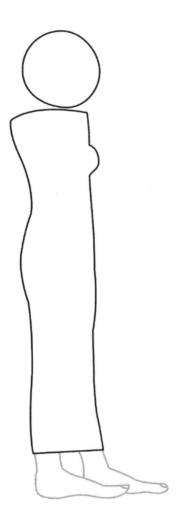

Add two legs to the profile under the skirt.

# Step 4.

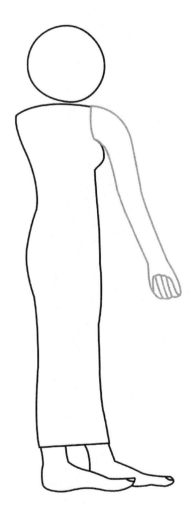

Draw a straight hand on the right.

# Step 5.

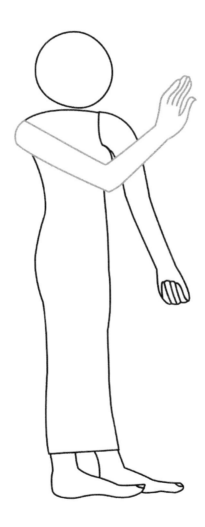

Draw a bent arm on the left, be close to the original.

25

# Step 6.

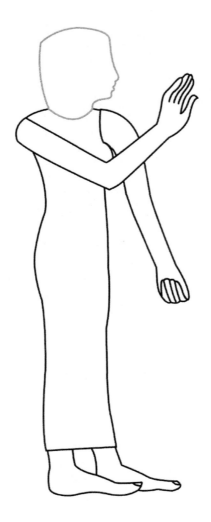

Draw the head in profile.

26

# Step 7.

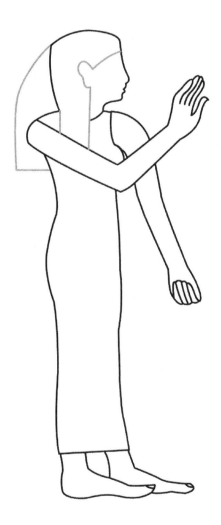

Add a hairstyle to the head.

27

# Step 8.

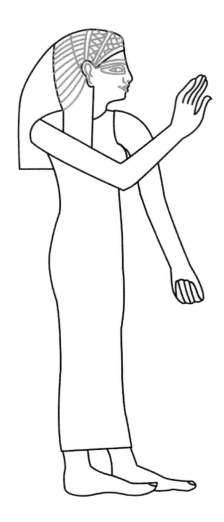

Add to the hairstyle jewelry, as shown in the example.

# Step 9.

Draw a hat.

# Step 10.

Add jewelry in the form of bracelets, necklaces and belts.

# Step 11.

Done, let's start coloring!

# Step 12.

Color picture using turquoise for dress and decorations, orange for skin and hat.

# Step 13.

Add some shadows and highlights to add volume.

# Step 14.

Colored version.

# How to draw Anubis

# Step 1.

Draw a small circle at the top of the head sheet.

# Step 2.

Draw an elongated face like a dog's and high pointed ears.

# Step 3.

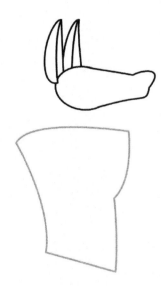

Draw a trapezoidal body just below the head.

# Step 4.

Draw a skirt just below the body.

# Step 5.

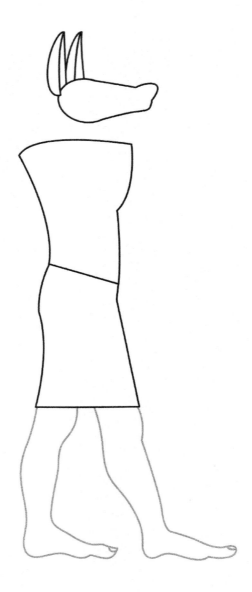

Add two legs to the profile under the skirt.

# Step 6.

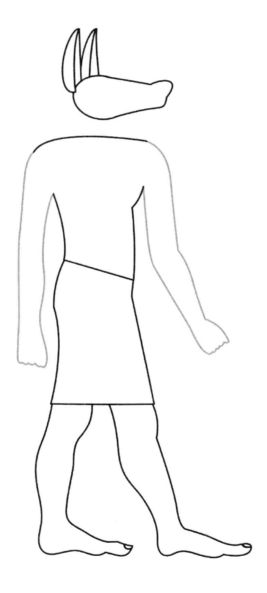

Add two hands on the sides of the body.

41

# Step 7.

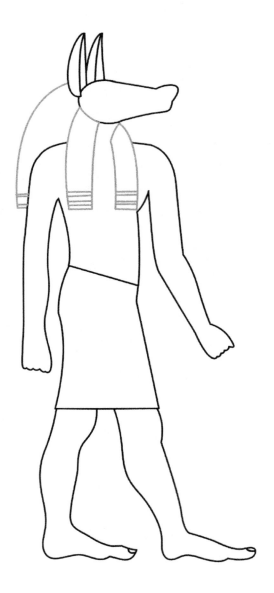

Draw a hairstyle, as shown in the example.

# Step 8.

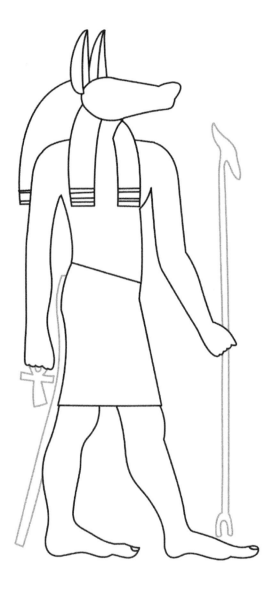

Draw a staff and ankh cross in the hands of Anubis, as well as a long strip from the waist to the heels.

# Step 9.

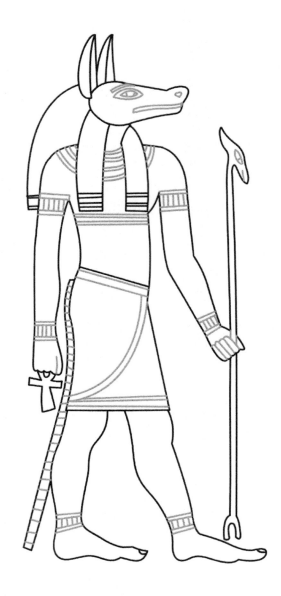

Add jewelry in the form of bracelets, necklaces, tunics and belts.

# Step 10.

Add folds on the skirt, stripes on the hair and scales on the tunic, as well as decoration on the belt.

# Step 11.

Done, let's start coloring!

# Step 12.

Color picture using brown for skin, yellow and red for skirt and decorations, blue for staff, eyes and mouth, violet for tunic.

# Step 13.

Add some shadows and highlights to add volume.

# Step 14.

Colored version.

# How to draw Osiris

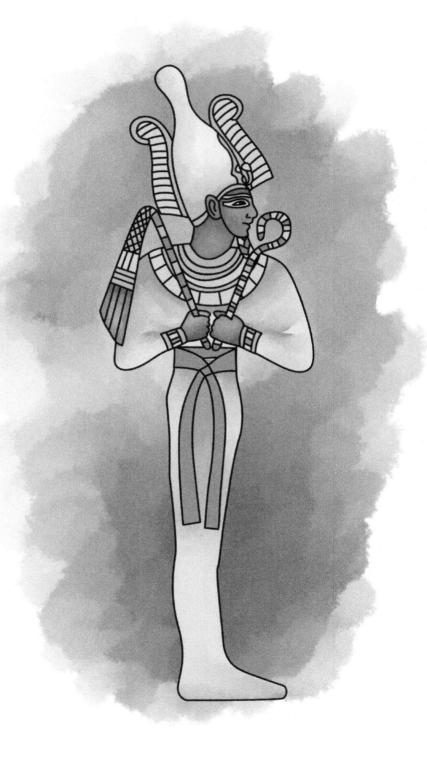

50

# Step 1.

Draw a small circle at the top of the head sheet.

# Step 2.

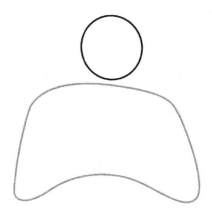

Draw a curved figure under the head for the upper body.

# Step 3.

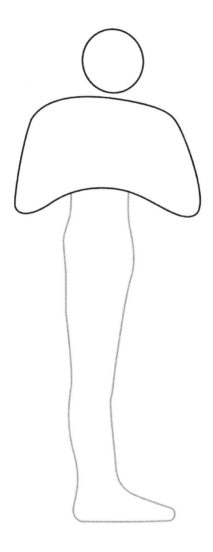

Draw the rest of the body with the legs in profile, be close to the original.

# Step 4.

Draw the face in profile and the fists folded on the chest.

# Step 5.

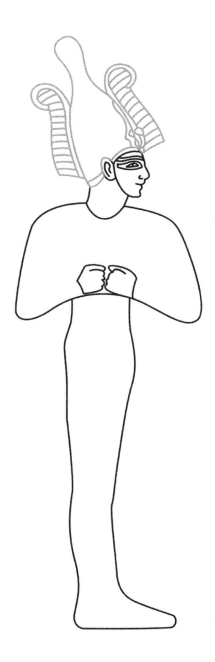

Draw a hat on the head, as shown in the example.

# Step 6.

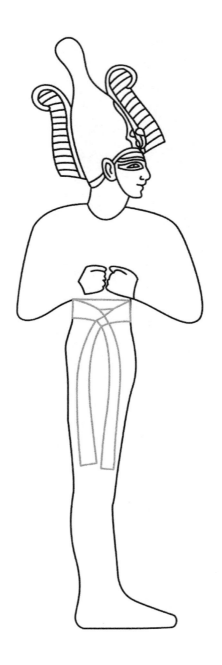

Add a belt to the dress.

# Step 7.

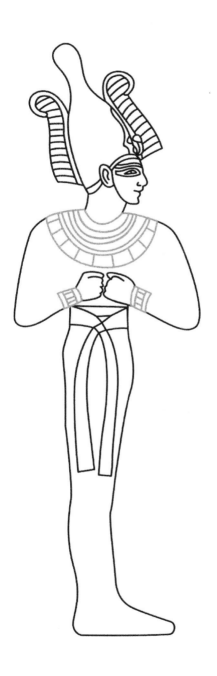

Add a necklace and bracelets.

# Step 8.

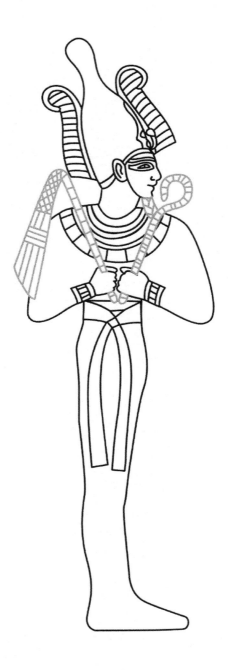

Draw in the hands of Osiris the attributes of the Egyptian god.

58

# Step 9.

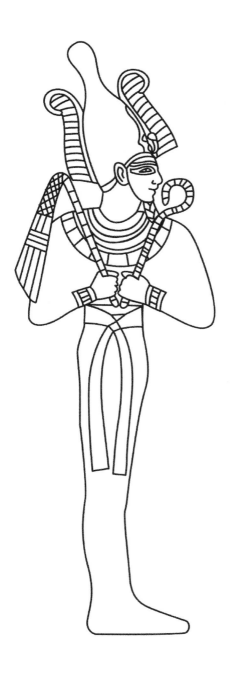

Done, let's start coloring!

# Step 10.

Color picture using orange for skin, yellow for hat, beige for dress, violet for belt, blue and gold for decorations and staff.

# Step 11.

Add some shadows and highlights to add volume.

# Step 12.

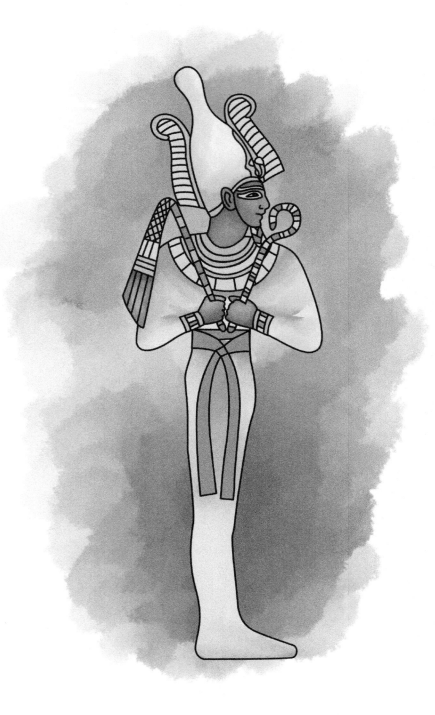

Colored version.

# How to draw Bastet

# Step 1.

Draw a small circle at the top of the head sheet.

# Step 2.

Draw a small trapezoidal body just below the head.

# Step 3.

Draw a long narrow skirt.

# Step 4.

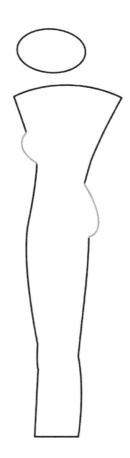

Add a couple of bulges as shown in the example.

# Step 5.

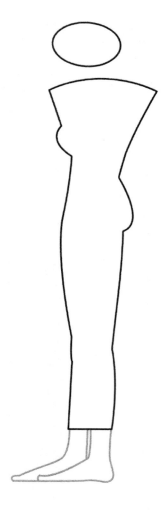

Draw a legs in profile.

# Step 6.

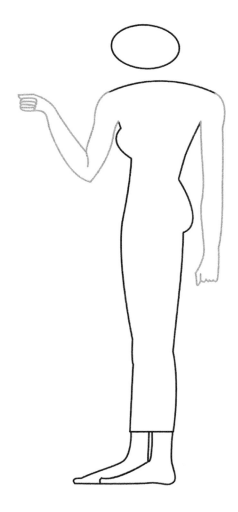

Draw two hands - one straight, the second bent.

# Step 7.

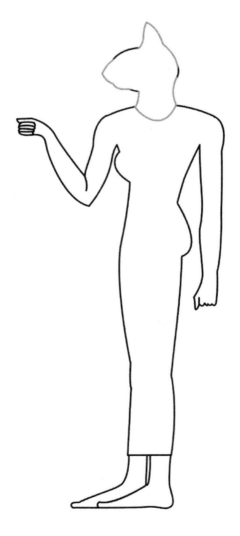

Draw the cat's head in profile.

# Step 8.

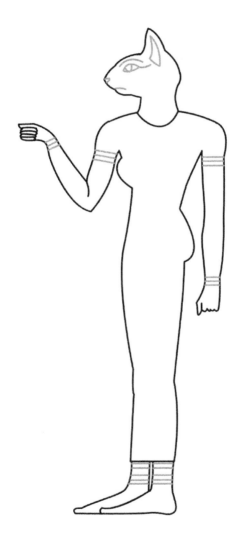

Add face and bracelets to the arms and legs.

71

# Step 9.

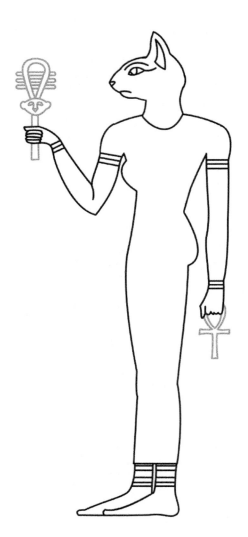

Add the attributes of the Egyptian god Bastet to the hands.

# Step 10.

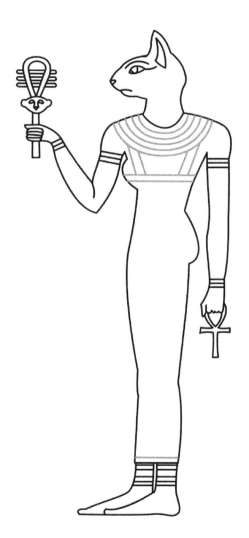

Draw a necklace and straps on the dress.

# Step 11.

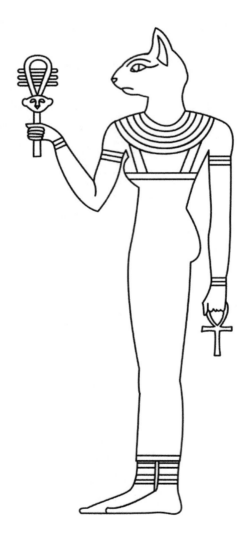

Done, let's start coloring!

# Step 12.

Color picture using white for dress, black for head, yellow for skin, blue and gold for decorations and staff.

# Step 13.

Add some shadows and highlights to add volume.

# Step 14.

Colored version.

# How to draw Ra

# Step 1.

Draw a small circle at the top of the head sheet.

# Step 2.

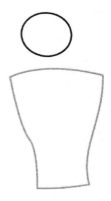

Draw a trapezoidal body just below the head.

# Step 3.

Draw a skirt just below the body.

# Step 4.

Add two legs to the profile under the skirt.

# Step 5.

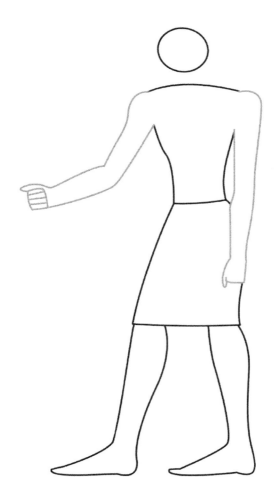

Draw two hands on the sides of the body, one straight, one bent.

# Step 6.

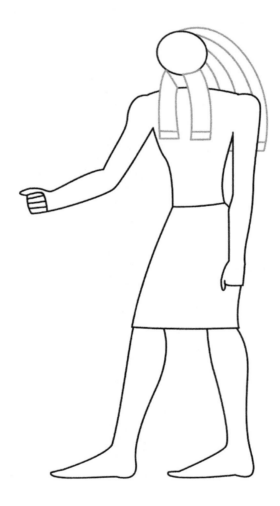

Draw a hairstyle as shown in the example.

# Step 7.

Draw the face of the bird in profile, a necklace and bracelets on his hands.

# Step 8.

Draw a tunic and stripes on the skirt.

86

# Step 9.

Draw a hat in the form of a large circle with a snake on top.

# Step 10.

Draw in the hands a staff, ankh cross and a long strip from the waist to the heels.

# Step 11.

Done, let's start coloring!

# Step 12.

Color picture using red for skin, white for skirt and face, orange for hat, green for hair and tunic.

# Step 13.

Add some shadows and highlights to add volume.

# Step 14.

Colored version.

# How to draw Amon-Ra

# Step 1.

Draw a small circle at the top of the head sheet.

# Step 2.

Draw a trapezoidal body just below the head.

# Step 3.

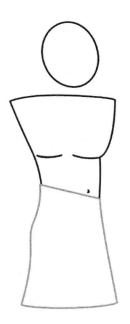

Draw a skirt just below the body.

# Step 4.

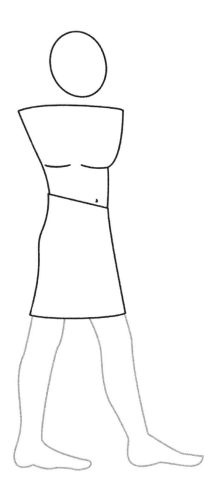

Add two legs to the profile under the skirt.

# Step 5.

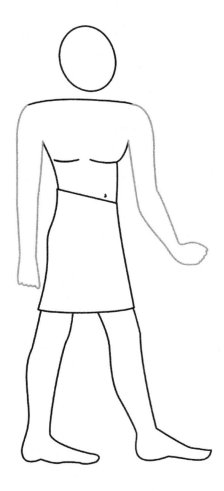

Draw two hands on the sides of the body, one straight, one bent.

# Step 6.

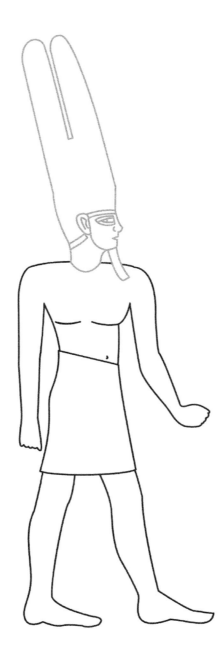

Draw a face in profile and a hat on the head, as shown in the example.

# Step 7.

Draw the details on the headdress and skirt, as well as a necklace and fingers.

# Step 8.

Draw a stick and ankh cross in hands.

# Step 9.

Done, let's start coloring!

# Step 10.

Color picture using orange for skin, yellow for face, necklace and hat, beige for skirt, wand and beard.

# Step 11.

Add some shadows and highlights to add volume.

104

# Step 12.

Colored version.

# About the Author

Andy Hopper is an American illustrator born in sunny California just a hair's breadth from the beautiful Sierra foothills. After studying Design and Media at UCLA, Andy decided to try his hand at teaching his own unique style of art to novice artists just starting out with their craft.

He has won numerous art awards and has several publications in print and e-book to his credit. His e-books teach the beginner artist how to draw using simple techniques suitable for all ages. While Andy prefers using chalk, pencil and pastels for his own artwork, but has been known to dabble in the world of watercolour from time to time and teach this skill to his students.

Andy Hopper lives just outside of Los Angeles in Santa Monica, California with his wife of 15 years and their three children. His art studio is a welcome respite to the area and he has been known to start impromptu outdoor art sessions with the people in his neighborhood for no charge.

Printed in Great Britain
by Amazon